This book belongs to:

....

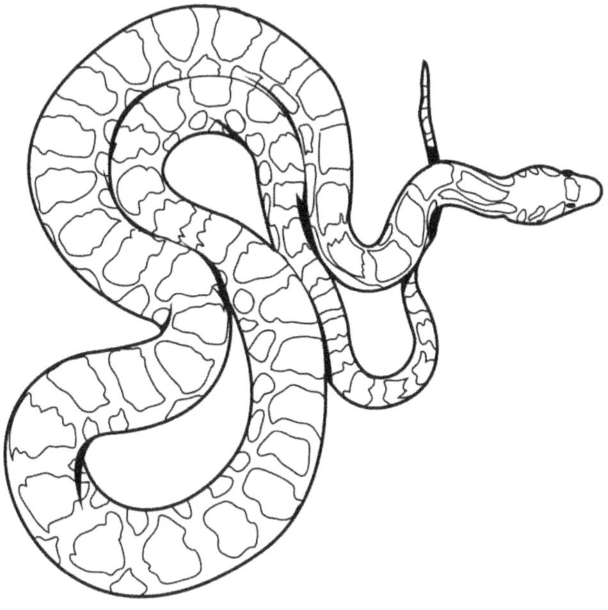

COLORING BOOK

COLOR TEST PAGE

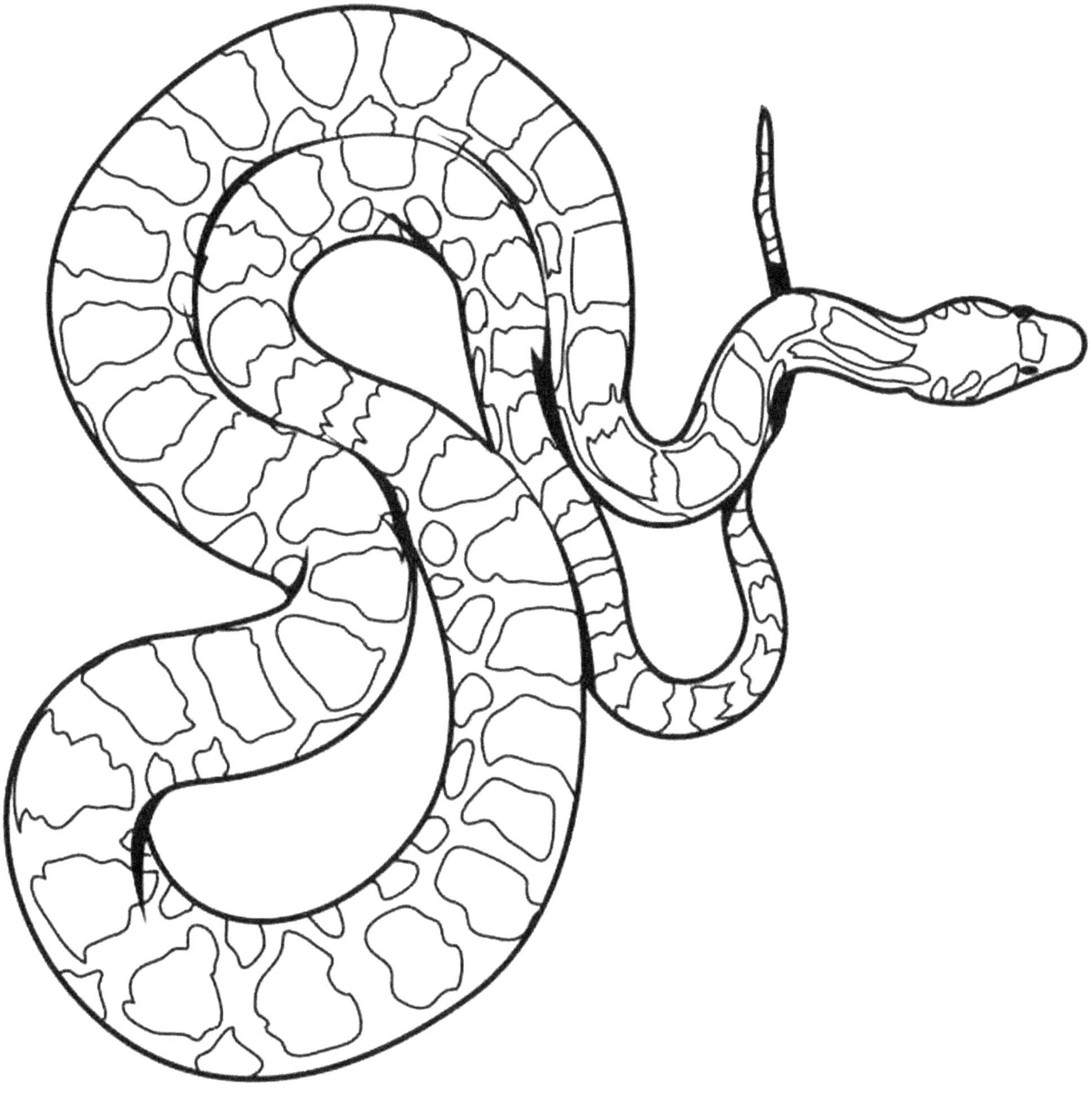

My Name

My Name

My Name

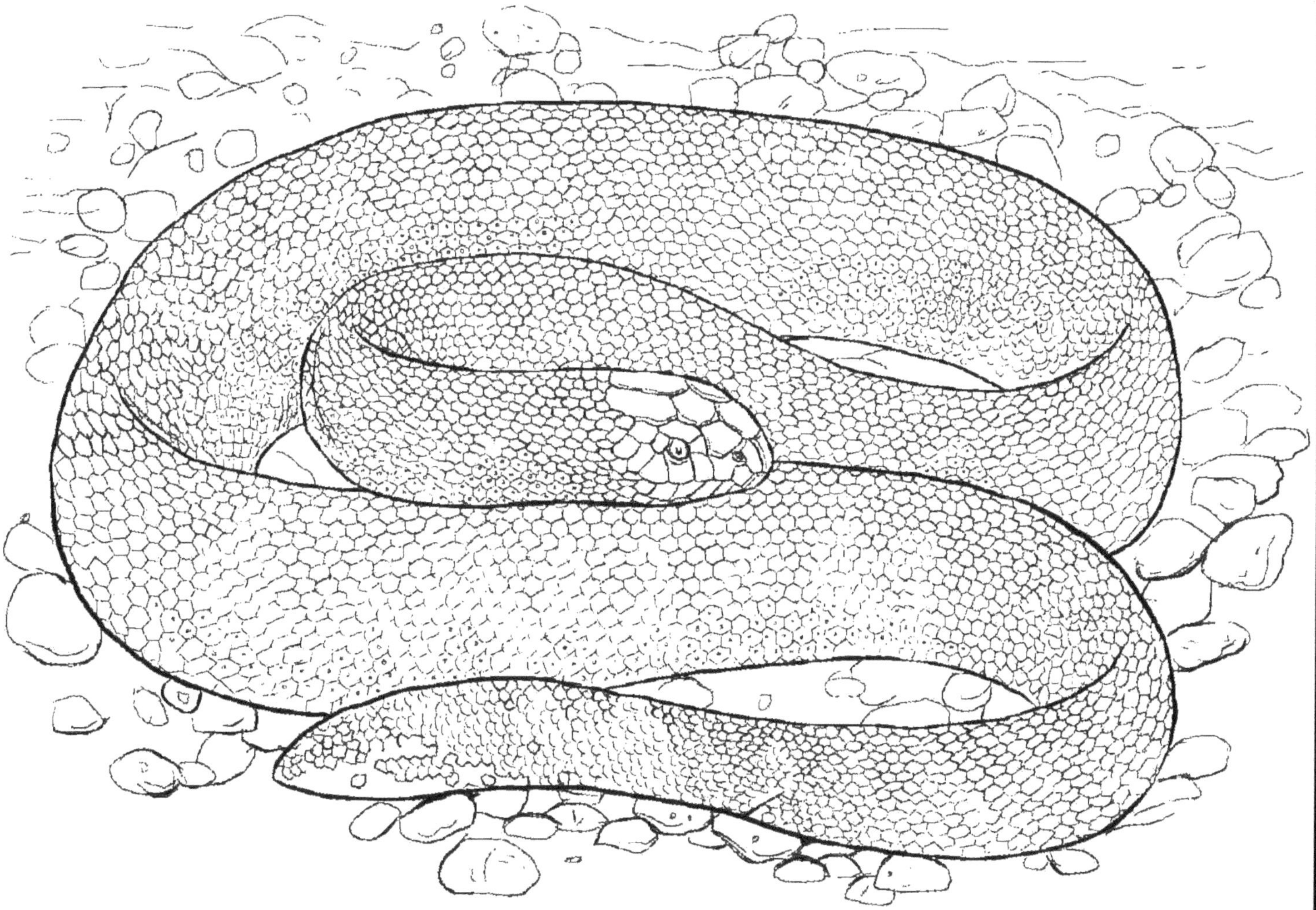

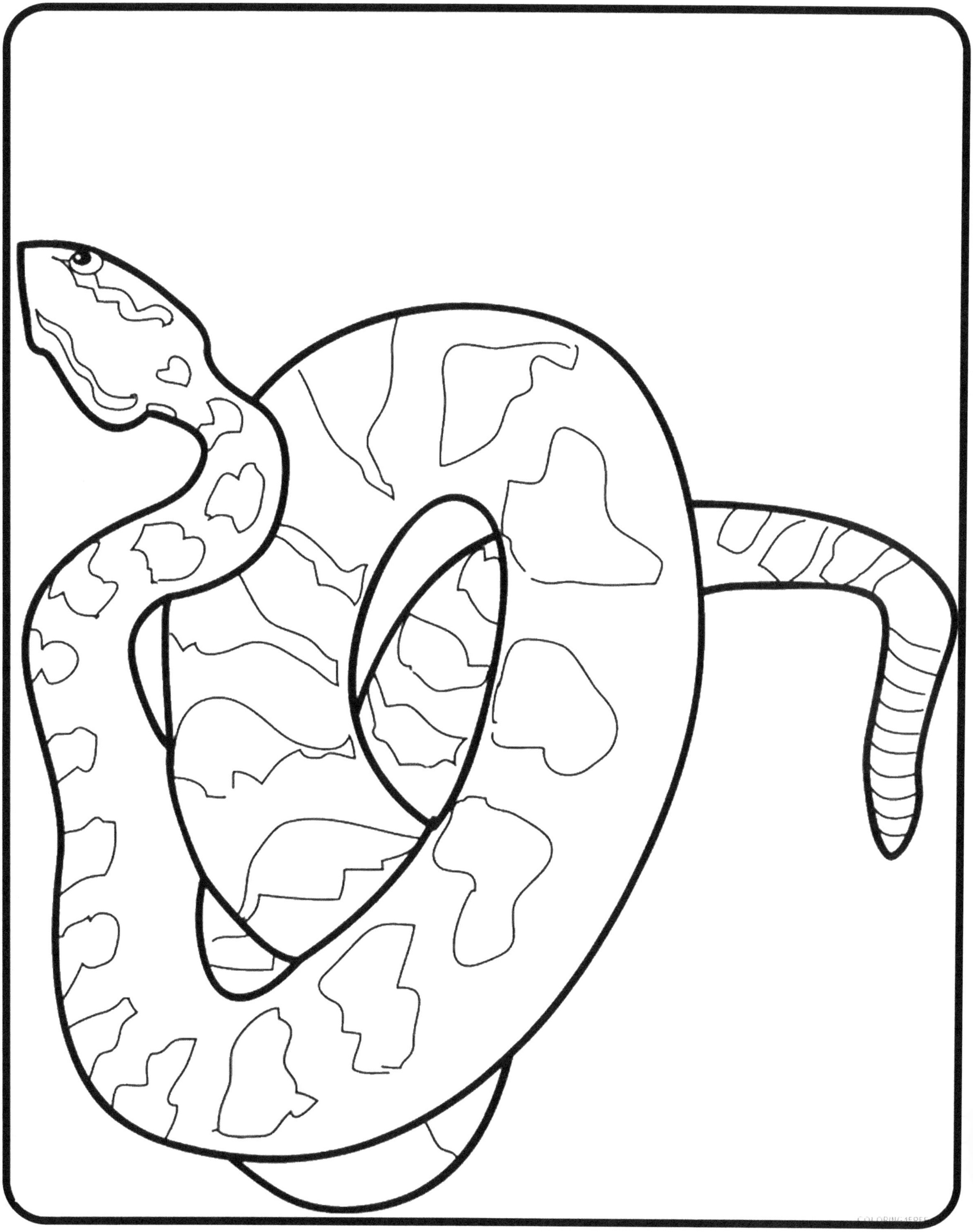

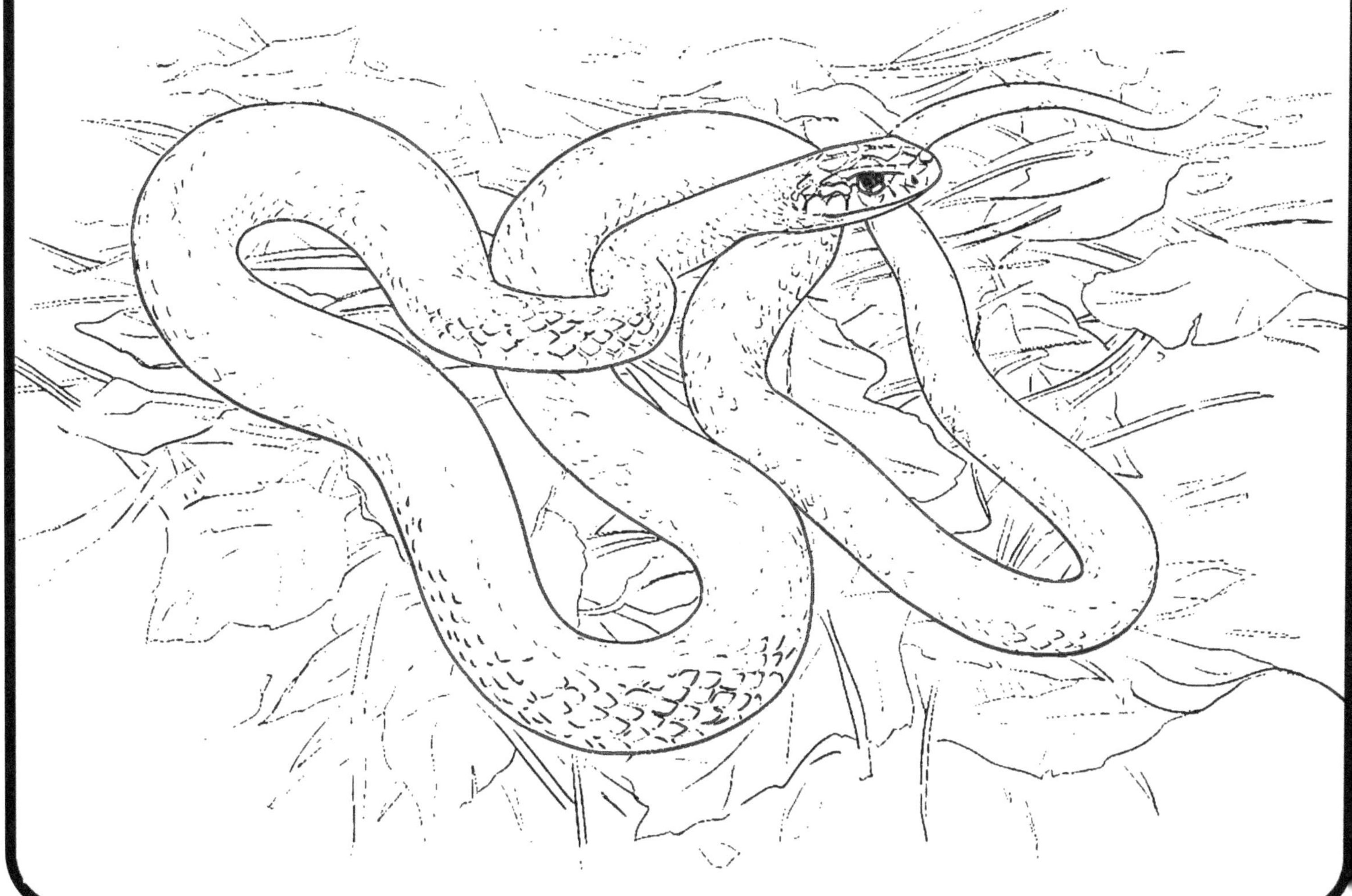

www.ingramcontent.com/pod-product-compliance
Lightning Source LLC
LaVergne TN
LVHW061738250225
804528LV00007B/738

* 9 7 9 8 3 2 1 4 5 0 7 8 9 *